THE POETRY OF FLEROVIUM

The Poetry of Flerovium

Walter the Educator

Silent King Books

SILENT KING BOOKS

SKB

Copyright © 2024 by Walter the Educator

All rights reserved. No part of this book may be reproduced in any manner whatsoever without written permission except in the case of brief quotations embodied in critical articles and reviews.

First Printing, 2024

Disclaimer
This book is a literary work; poems are not about specific persons, locations, situations, and/or circumstances unless mentioned in a historical context. This book is for entertainment and informational purposes only. The author and publisher offer this information without warranties expressed or implied. No matter the grounds, neither the author nor the publisher will be accountable for any losses, injuries, or other damages caused by the reader's use of this book. The use of this book acknowledges an understanding and acceptance of this disclaimer.

"Earning a degree in chemistry changed my life!"
– Walter the Educator

dedicated to all the chemistry lovers, like myself, across the world

FLEROVIUM

There lies a treasure, rare and divine,

FLEROVIUM

Flerovium, a jewel in the periodic line.

FLEROVIUM

Born in labs where scientists dream,

FLEROVIUM

A fleeting existence, a shimmering gleam,

FLEROVIUM

Synthesized with precision and care,

FLEROVIUM

Flerovium emerges, beyond compare.

FLEROVIUM

In the heart of a star, where pressures ignite,

FLEROVIUM

Elements fuse in the cosmic night,

FLEROVIUM

Amongst the chaos and fusion's embrace,

FLEROVIUM

Flerovium forms in a celestial race.

FLEROVIUM

With electrons swirling in quantum delight,

FLEROVIUM

Flerovium's essence, a mysterious sight,

FLEROVIUM

Its nucleus packed with protons galore,

FLEROVIUM

A testament to science's exploration encore.

FLEROVIUM

From the depths of the periodic chart,

FLEROVIUM

Flerovium emerges, a work of art,

FLEROVIUM

Its properties shrouded in scientific mist,

FLEROVIUM

A puzzle to solve, a riddle to twist.

FLEROVIUM

Unstable and short-lived, it defies control,

FLEROVIUM

A fleeting glimpse of a cosmic stroll,

FLEROVIUM

Yet in its brief moment, it leaves a mark,

FLEROVIUM

A testament to human intellect's spark.

FLEROVIUM

Its name, a tribute to Flerov's name,

FLEROVIUM

A pioneer of science, his legacy aflame,

FLEROVIUM

In laboratories, minds do delve,

FLEROVIUM

To unlock the secrets Flerovium does shelve.

FLEROVIUM

In the crucible of curiosity's fire,

FLEROVIUM

Scientists push boundaries, aim higher,

FLEROVIUM

Exploring the mysteries of the atomic sea,

FLEROVIUM

Flerovium whispers, "Come, discover me."

FLEROVIUM

From the depths of the Earth to the stars above,

FLEROVIUM

Flerovium beckons with a siren's love,

FLEROVIUM

A promise of knowledge, of truth untold,

FLEROVIUM

In its atomic dance, mysteries unfold.

FLEROVIUM

So let us raise a toast to Flerovium's name,

FLEROVIUM

To the scientists who play in science's game,

FLEROVIUM

For in the realm of elements, rare and profound,

FLEROVIUM

Flerovium's beauty will forever astound.

FLEROVIUM

ABOUT THE CREATOR

Walter the Educator is one of the pseudonyms for Walter Anderson. Formally educated in Chemistry, Business, and Education, he is an educator, an author, a diverse entrepreneur, and he is the son of a disabled war veteran. "Walter the Educator" shares his time between educating and creating. He holds interests and owns several creative projects that entertain, enlighten, enhance, and educate, hoping to inspire and motivate you.

Follow, find new works, and stay up to date with Walter the Educator™
at WaltertheEducator.com

www.ingramcontent.com/pod-product-compliance
Lightning Source LLC
LaVergne TN
LVHW051922060526
838201LV00060B/4128